MINDFUL MENTALITY

PERSEVERANCE

BY MARI SCHUH

BLUE OWL
BOOKS

TIPS FOR CAREGIVERS

Social and emotional learning (SEL) helps children connect with their emotions and gain a better understanding of themselves. Mindfulness can support this learning and help them develop a kind and inclusive mentality. By incorporating mindfulness and SEL into early learning, students can establish this mentality early and be better equipped to build strong connections and communities.

BEFORE READING

Talk to the student about perseverance. Discuss some real-life examples.

Discuss: What does perseverance mean to you? What are some other words or terms for perseverance? Talk about a time when you showed perseverance. What challenges did you face? What did you do?

AFTER READING

Talk to the student about practicing perseverance.

Discuss: How do you feel when you work toward a goal? How do you overcome setbacks? Talk about ways you can show perseverance at home and at school.

SEL GOAL

Talk with students about their goals. Explain that setting a goal and a date to complete it by can help them achieve it. Help them come up with ideas to check their progress. Maybe it is a calendar or journal. Some students may prefer weekly calendars, while others might like short, simple lists. Also discuss ways students can help one another with their goals and dreams. How can they be helpful, supportive friends and classmates?

TABLE OF CONTENTS

CHAPTER 1

WHAT IS PERSEVERANCE?

Maria is building a small machine. Her first plan did not work. Instead of giving up, she tries another plan.

Maria keeps trying even when it is hard. She gets **frustrated** and sometimes wants to give up. But she doesn't. This is **perseverance**. After a lot of hard work, she makes her machine run!

Persevering means not giving up during tough times. It means continuing to try and work even when things are difficult.

Why should we persevere? It helps us learn and grow. You might not reach every **goal**. But by working hard, you'll learn to have **grit**. You'll learn to do your best no matter what. When the next challenge comes, you'll be ready!

SET GOOD GOALS

Setting goals can help you be **resilient**. But don't set goals that are too big. Is your goal possible to **achieve**? **Focus** on what you can do today to achieve it.

CHAPTER 2

WHAT PERSEVERANCE LOOKS LIKE

Jake and his brother fight a lot. Jake wants to find a way to get along. He keeps trying. He asks his brother to play a new game. It works! They have fun.

Avery got a new puppy. She wants it to do tricks. But the puppy doesn't know any yet. It needs time to learn. Avery works hard to be **patient**. She doesn't give up teaching him. They practice every day.

Griffin doesn't understand some of the words in the book he is reading. He gets frustrated. But he reminds himself that learning takes time. He looks up words he doesn't know in a dictionary. It helps him become a stronger reader!

USE MINDFULNESS

Remember that everyone learns at his or her own pace. Be patient with yourself. If you feel frustrated, take a break. You can use **mindfulness** to calm down. Breathe slowly. How are you feeling? Then think about your strengths. You can do this!

Perseverance helps us in many ways. Jody's grandpa is very sick. She is scared about what will happen to him, but she tries to stay positive. She visits him every day and draws pictures for him. This helps her **cope** with her grandpa's illness.

CHAPTER 3

KEEP GOING

When Lucy misses a goal in the game, she starts to cry. She takes a quick break to get her head back in the game. Afterward, she talks about her **emotions** with her coach. Talking helps Lucy feel better.

Oliver's goal is to win the spelling bee next month. Today, he had a **setback** when he struggled with a spelling test. Setbacks are OK. Oliver is resilient and doesn't quit. He keeps studying.

Do you have big dreams for the future? Goals can help you make them real. Lisa dreams of being a scientist. She sets a goal to get an A in science all year. She focuses on her schoolwork.

MAKE A PLAN

Think about when you want to complete your goal. Is it this week? Or is it this month? Set a date. Then keep track of how far you've come. You'll see how well you're doing.

When you need help, talk to an adult you trust. It can be hard to share your feelings. Remember that everyone needs help. People who care for you will listen. They will help and **encourage** you. They can help give you the **confidence** and patience you need to keep going!

Ria made a new friend at school. She uses sign language. Ria wants to learn to sign, too! Why? So she can talk with her new friend. Ria practices each day.

Persevering is hard work, but it is the key to meeting your goals. You can do great things when you persevere!

GOALS AND TOOLS

GROW WITH GOALS

There are many ways we can persevere. Practice with these goals.

Goal: Think about a time you didn't give up. What challenges did you face? What did you learn from those challenges?

Goal: Read a book or story about someone who has shown perseverance. Share what you've learned with a friend.

Goal: Write down ways you can show perseverance at school and at home. What can you do each day to reach these goals?

MINDFULNESS EXERCISE

Mindfulness can help you persevere. When you're upset and want to quit, try this breathing exercise.

1. Close your eyes. Slowly breathe in and out. Focus on your breathing.

2. Place your fingertips together, making a sphere with your hands.

3. When you breathe in, move your fingertips apart, making the sphere bigger. When you breathe out, bring them back together, making the sphere smaller. Continue this exercise until you feel relaxed and focused.

GLOSSARY

achieve
To do something successfully after making an effort.

confidence
A feeling of self-assuredness and a strong belief in your own abilities.

cope
To deal with something effectively.

emotions
Feelings, such as happiness, sadness, or anger.

encourage
To give someone confidence, usually by using praise and support.

focus
To concentrate on something.

frustrated
Angry and annoyed.

goal
Something you aim to do.

grit
Passion for and perseverance toward long-term goals.

mindfulness
A mentality achieved by focusing on the present moment and calmly recognizing and accepting your feelings, thoughts, and sensations.

patient
Able to put up with problems or delays without getting angry or upset.

perseverance
The act of continuing to do or try something even if you have difficulties.

resilient
Able to recover easily from misfortune or change.

setback
A problem that delays you or keeps you from making progress.

TO LEARN MORE

FACT SURFER

Finding more information is as easy as 1, 2, 3.

1. Go to www.factsurfer.com

2. Enter "**perseverance**" into the search box.

3. Choose your cover to see a list of websites.

INDEX

Blue Owl Books are published by Jump!, 5357 Penn Avenue South, Minneapolis, MN 55419, www.jumplibrary.com

Copyright © 2021 Jump! International copyright reserved in all countries. No part of this book may be reproduced in any form without written permission from the publisher.

Library of Congress Cataloging-in-Publication Data

Names: Schuh, Mari C., 1975– author.
Title: Perseverance / by Mari Schuh.
Description: [Minneapolis]: [Jump!, Inc.], 2021. | Series: Mindful mentality
Includes index. | Audience: Ages 7–10 | Audience: Grades 2–3
Identifiers: LCCN 2020000315 (print)
LCCN 2020000316 (ebook)
ISBN 9781645273868 (library binding)
ISBN 9781645273875 (paperback)
ISBN 9781645273882 (ebook)
Subjects: LCSH: Perseverance (Ethics)–Juvenile literature. | Mindfulness (Psychology)–Juvenile literature.
Classification: LCC BJ1533.P4 S377 2021 (print)
LCC BJ1533.P4 (ebook) | DDC 155.2/5–dc23
LC record available at https://lccn.loc.gov/2020000315
LC ebook record available at https://lccn.loc.gov/2020000316

Editor: Jenna Gleisner
Designer: Molly Ballanger

Photo Credits: Creativa Images/Shutterstock, cover; Sergey Novikov/Shutterstock, 1; Apollofoto/Shutterstock, 3; M_a_y_a/iStock, 4, 5; JGI/Jamie Grill/Getty, 6–7; Luis Molinero/Shutterstock, 8; kali9/iStock, 9; PeopleImages/iStock, 10–11; Ridofranz/iStock, 12–13; Fuse/Getty, 14; Flashon Studio/Shutterstock, 15; Twinsterphoto/Shutterstock, 16–17; mihailomilovanovic/iStock, 18–19; BRIAN MITCHELL/Getty, 20–21.

Printed in the United States of America at Corporate Graphics in North Mankato, Minnesota.